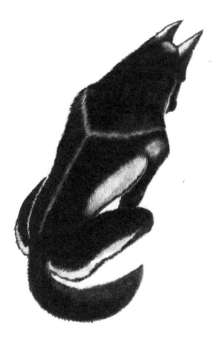

bookvault
Publishing

Take It As Red

ISBN: 9781804672648
Perfect Bound

First published in 2023 by bookvault Publishing,
Peterborough, United Kingdom

An Environmentally friendly book printed and bound in
England by bookvault, powered by
printondemand-worldwide

Dear Ania

ill write this CLEARLY FOR
YOU ... :-

Thanks for all your
support!

Best wishes

79/102

TAKE IT AS RED
A book of poetry by Paul Giffney

This first book is dedicated to everyone who has ever heard me read a poem aloud, who has ever helped me with a poem, who has ever introduced me to a poem or who was kind enough to share their poetry with me♥.

Thank you.

_____

♥ Especially my mother, my husband and the poets of Northamptonshire – love to you all.

FOREWORD

by *That Joe Payne*

As a long-standing critically acclaimed Progressive Rock singer, composer and lyricist, there is one thing I daren't title myself: *a poet.*

I suppose that's because I admire poetry as an artform that requires so much more than just a catchy hook. But there's no real way for me to decipher what qualities make for a good poem, really. All I know is that I look up to anyone that can inspire broader feeling and thought through words alone.

Mr Paul Giffney, however, should certainly award himself such a title; not that he needs to, as our town already did, deservingly crowning him our Bard of Northampton in recent years!

In all of Northampton - the town with the biggest population in Europe, so I'm told – there's no one I know throughout its thriving scene of arts and culture that can compete with or rival Paul's exuberant personality. To meet him, you will discover his enthusiasm is contagious. Good luck finding anyone else as encouraging, supportive, willing and, well, vocal. I suppose, those features, along with his poetic talents, are the reason why he made such a great Bard, combining his best attributes to lead other chaotic-in-nature artists to water, and bring out the best in the community around him.

I too have felt the supportive embrace of Paul, who welcomely insists on aiding me wherever he can in the promotion of my own work. Perhaps another interview about an upcoming release on his NLive radio show, or even just supporting my events by being there. It all goes very much noticed, and I appreciate his friendship greatly.

And what of his poetry?

Let me tell you, this gentleman's engaging delivery is one to be envied. Most Wednesdays, whether I choose to or not, I find myself listening intently to his monologues at my local pub's weekly open mics. A smutty humour often decorates his perfectly phrased, reflective pieces. In the same way that someone might impulsively chuckle after delivering some bad news, this man seems to clearly understand that all emotions are linked with complexity. It would be a cliché to say there is no dark without light, and yet for so many creators this balance is a tricky recipe to get right. (Ooh, that rhymes!)

I see his influence in so many others. People who I once knew as shy and quietly alternative have been dragged out of their shells as they dip their toes in poetic expression. Free to say what they want, how they want. Allowed to feel safe and confident in the same environment as one another. I'd be lucky to find this anywhere else and count myself fortunate to have such a treasure on my doorstep.

So, have a read through these delightful poems. When I do, I can hear Paul's voice reading them aloud, having witnessed so many of these performed in person. Some will make you laugh, while others might make you sad, but what they all seem to do for me is scratch under the surface of everything we see in society. Cynical, amusing, and not at all trivial! I'm very flattered to be asked to write this foreword, particularly as a heavily dyslexic person who doesn't read much. That reminds me: this would make a great audiobook! [**Note from the author:** an audio version will be made available for owners of this book: www.paulgiffney.uk/poetry]

Love,

That Joe Payne

THAT JOE PAYNE is a classically trained vocalist with backgrounds in prog, pop, and rock music, remembered by audiences for his impressive **five-octave** range alongside some spectacular showmanship.

The singer has released no less than fourteen albums with various artists since his career began in 2011. As well as producing solo material, Payne's collaborations include work with *John Holden, Zio, Methexis*, and *The Enid*.

Personal achievements include being voted Best Male Vocalist for two years running (2014 & 2015) in the *Prog Magazine* Readers' Poll. He also received three *Progressive Music Award* nominations in 2013 and 2015 for his work with *The Enid*, including Best Band, Best Album, and Best Event.

For more information on them, and to buy his amazing work, visit his website: www.thatjoepayne.com

Author's Introduction

Alice Christiana Thompson Meynell – poet, critic and essayist – wrote how "red has been praised for its nobility as the colour of life."[1] This is a book that gathers some of my first poems written whilst living in the town where the motto *Castello Fortior Concordia* echoes amongst ruined castle walls.

I became a bard in 2019, just as Covid-19 was brewing in the bellies of bats. Not much longer after I had received a blue cloak and the ability to engage the public, to help entertain and communicate messages of the people to the people was I, amongst every other person in the country (bar those in politics), put into Lockdown. Restricted, my words festered and gathered, swimming in a brain that was beleaguered with depression, undiagnosed-at-the-time ADHD, and cyclothymia (a bi-polar condition that makes mood swings more of a random roller-coaster). I was stuck. I toyed with the idea of a book but didn't have enough material. I was encouraged to write by many people though, by the creative spirit (or *Awen*) of the world – but I couldn't. I struggled. I then hosted a radio show and helped others create and stretch their wings. Slowly, words returned to my pen. Some of those poems, the ones marked '#' in the section titled "Red Tape", are the ones that I thought apt for this book.

Because this book is just the beginning.

---

[1] Meynell, Alice Christiana Thompson, 1847-1922. The Colour of Life: And Other Essays On Things Seen And Heard. 3d ed. London: Lane, 1896.

There are many "colours of life" and as Meynell later explains in her essay, "the true colour of life is the colour of the body, the colour of the covered red, the implicit and not explicit red of the living heart and the pulses."

I found that my poems started fitting into coloured 'sections'; collections that will start to emerge in the next few years and ultimately create a collection of work.

Do I think these poems are good enough to publish? Yes. I teach English Literature sometimes and have found myself smiling when I hold these poems and realise that *I* wrote them. I forget sometimes, you see. A brain is a weird thing and weirder is when it doesn't recall its own creations, especially when they're definitely yours, scribbled in notebooks and on mead-spattered papers, scraps of text in a phone and, most importantly, echoing in ears from previous open-mic nights. And therein lies the rub. How do I introduce my poems? Should I *have* to?

I don't think so, and yet there is the entertainment spectacle of spoken word for a lot of these poems, the performance aspect of the poet – the bard is more than just a written poet in my opinion: they need to engage a crowd with the inflections, the sounds, the volume and intonations of the spoken word as well as have something viable to say. So how do I speak to you, right *now*?

Well, I'm going to do a quick introduction to most (not all) of the poems that I would perform on a stage (usually the Black Prince public house back room) so you can also sit there and listen. *If* you want to.

You don't have to. You can go straight to the poems right now, and I don't mind. They are a different text when read alone and hence I've only included those I think strong enough to stand without an introduction. A title explained isn't, for me, doing its job. Yet the last poem of this collection, I have explored this idea in more depth, writing notes in a TS. Eliot-style – to explore this further.

I have enjoyed writing them. I hope you enjoy reading them.

~ " Hi, I'm Paul... " ~

PAINTING THE TOWN RED is the first set of poems in this book aka the 'Bardic' collection. They are poems to do with my being the 10th Bard of Northampton; they relate to finding my poetic voice and are the poems that I sometimes use to 'warm up' or 'read' a crowd. Most bardic shenanigans and events happen amongst public houses or festivals, despite a movement away from pubs. Yet we still cannot move too far from the stereotypical imagery of the bawdy 'bard' it seems.

By beginning with *Participation*, I hope to set the tone - establishing how any poem or performed piece on a stage is a partnership between audience and performer. With both being a undeterminable variable, each performance is unique to that day. A poem in print therefore removes one variable – this book won't change. You, dear reader, will though. The eye alters, alters all and thus this (and every book) will never be the same river twice. Time will flow and I hope this poem summarises that (don't worry, the rest of the introductions will be much shorter).

Be... and *P...* are both poems that play with poetic terms and the idea of poetry. The pretention of poetry annoys me – I want it to be accessible for everyone and do my best to make this happen. These poems, in part, comment on that.

Reading An Audience is about the work a performer does to adapt their set – who are you, reader, holding this book right now? Unlike performing for a crowd, I cannot alter the set order now. But you can still bounce around the book as you see fit. Do. Remember though that a live audience is being judged by the performer as equally as them judging the act!

Mingling is my husband's favourite of this collection – I wrote it, partly for him and partly for every introvert out there. I took a long reflection upon the nature of extroversion and how society is focused mostly on one group and not the other – I use the extended metaphor of the kid's party as something relatable to everyone.

A Pregnant Pause is my nod to every writer and creator out there – we hate the block, and I thought I'd make the process of creation a little more graphic...

RED TAPE is the bane of society but can also hinder processes that shouldn't be rushed as well. Ultimately though, my spontaneous nature always creates the serpentine imagery of the bureaucracy that strangles most creativity out there.

NHS Stealing was the poem I wrote for a meeting where I was invited to help give some 'creativity' to a meeting of NHS officials – whether or not it worked, I don't know, but I know the poem's tone was appreciated by all the hard workers there!

Pink Pounded! Is my cynical take on consumerism during special 'times' of the equal rights calendars whilst *The Second Key Stage* tries to encapsulate the awareness I have of education and its power. Or lack thereof. My Covid-19 poems that I wrote in lockdown, *Anxious Bliss* and *Distances in Social Media* are sandwich slices around *Will You Belong?* – a poem that I wrote for one of the bardic competitions in Northampton. All look at society in different ways, all explore my thoughts on distance, closeness and the 'poetical proxemics' that dance between these interactions. *Pathogen of Least Resistance* however just looks at the results of this country's poor responses to the pandemic.

Unity finalises this section with its contempt for the ideas of segregation in our society; my loathing for forms being hopefully apparent to the readers by now!

RED ON YOU focuses on the bloodier aspects of my life – we start with a poem subtitled *Scales: Skin and Sound.* The actual title is revealed in the naming of the content, which in turn provides, in a circular fashion, the focus of the title. Thus, we loop back on ourselves. It's the one I enjoy performing most, but the next is a poem that I enjoy introducing most: "I wrote this next poem as a thank you to my husband, a man who I love dearly and appreciate more each day. It's called *Parasites.*" I love watching the passive interaction of the audience as the poem progresses as well...

Samaritans is a piece that I wrote as a request for a friend whose colleague volunteers for this great charity. That person thought, after a particular long night, that they had achieved little. I wrote this response and now actively encourage anyone who reads it to donate, if they can, to the cause. 116123 is the phone number in the UK to call – and they answer every hour of every day.

Brothers explores the adage that blood is thicker than water whilst *Stickers* examines the ideas of self-reward. My current personal trainer, James, now rewards me with stickers every time I go after I explained how we all seek validation in our lives - this poem is a partial acknowledgement and tribute to everyone who has ever pushed and supported me, including an awareness of my own drive.

SEEING RED brings together the last topic of this collection, four poems of anger and reveals, if not already, my liberal political views. Violence doesn't solve anything – the talking afterwards does – but the building up of tension needs a valve, and soon. I have my words, but all the poems in this collection ask about this tension. The first *There's a crack...* is a dig at power whilst both *There's No I in Team* and *Competition* explore LGBTQIA+ issues.

It is a long journey that we are all on, but one in which the Trickster often sits aside, challenging us all to a game of *Thimblerig*; the last poem in this collection that has also accompanying notes. Why? Not just to explore a style of T.S. Eliot but to explore this idea overall of giving answers, or some answers at least, to some meaning of a poem. Again, your choice if you want to read them. Or not. 😊

Safe journeys to you all and see you in the next book!

Paul Giffney, Imbolc, 2023.

ABOUT THE AUTHOR

PAUL GIFFNEY was born in North Devon, England in the late 1970s. He has been a lover of poetry ever since the day that he discovered Spike Milligan's *On the Ning Nang Nong* (and he still enjoys reciting it today).

He performs his own poetry, and others, at many open mic nights across the country and on his radio show called *County Culture*. Paul lives in Northampton with his husband, his cat and a pile of books that do not fit on any shelf. (The books. The cat fits on every shelf).

More information can be found on his website: www.paulgiffney.uk

PAINTING THE TOWN RED

"Whenever there was any excitement or anybody got particularly loud, they always said somebody was 'painting the town red'."

The Boston Journal (November 1884 edition)

Participation

Hello boys and girls and others – are you sitting or standing
comfortably? Good. Remember that.
For when a storyteller, such as myself, sits and tells a story,
you take part...

You listen. – You may learn.
You picture. – You may burn
The words of a story into your head
Told by a teller either living or dead.
The word of a narrator, beginning a tale
A serpent or dragon, a flagon of ale,
A cave, a castle, a princess, a prince
A fairy-tale romance, a traveller with hints
Of a future that's brighter, not orange... but blue
(Because rhyming is not always an easy thing to do)
Taking part is the key to a door I will show
But only you can open it, close it, or go.
How does this work? We need to take *a part;*
This participation – let's go from the start:
Recall the inclusion, the use of address
Direct to the audience, remove the distress
Encourage to join in, to involve, to belong
(An echo from times past – but that's another song.)
We participate, daily, sign and tick boxes
Of forms, in letters and on petitions for foxes...
But *they* do not listen, they don't partake
Of our world and our thoughts but is it our mistake?
To participate daily, to create pictures true
Yet read fake understandings, me sharing to you;

An audience now listening and burning my words
Direct into meanings until there are birds.
But don't listen to wizards and experts and truth;
Like and share stories; reject the gospel of Ruth.
Ignore other stories from lands of afar.
The heavens are wide yet people only followed one star.
Religion and fable, both need you to take part
To listen to words, to take them to heart.
The soldier grasps at what they can take,
The scholar missing what history might fake,
The parent and child repeating the tale,
The loner recalling pasts over flagons of ale.
New bards arrive and tell of new tales
Of lands and of monsters, of ships and of whales.
They combine with others; their stories are telling,
Yet they're made now for profit and only for selling.
Our stories known wider, on film and on screen;
We Marvel at stories that once were obscene.
Less care is given, and we take part less
Our stories made simpler, Mice clean up the mess.
Participate and get what you want
Don't complain if you get what you need,
Because the taking of a part from the whole
Makes the whole weak and causes all to bleed.
Are you still sitting or standing comfortably?
Are you still participating?
Are you still?
Take apart your taking part,
And tell *your* story to others with heart.

BE IS FOR BARD

The bard, deciding upon pretentious third person starts:
Light the candle. Light the incense.
The mood is now created. Purple pen. Fluffy carpet.
(Ignore the parasites) Distraction.
After all, people need to focus
(Neighbours arrive. Car door closes. Doors open. Laughter. Focus)
Pen picked up. Pause.

Not writer's block. Pretention is examined.
A poem about picking up a pen?!
"What does it mean?"
Can the cigar-shaped writing implement just *be* that?
The bard pauses. / Again.
Why does art have to be 'other' than art?
An arrangement of chosen medium alone: voice forming phoneme,
ink forming grapheme, paint on a palette, shoe on a foot,
movement of a foot, turning of a ring.

Can this just 'be'? Not be a thing. But be?

Not the first to say or write this. Quick. Resist the urge to
critique/compare this.
Romantic, modern, epic, essay; poetic laurels on display.

Be.
Breathe.
Write.

The bard decides the next step.
No defence of poetry or poesie here. Just words.
The plosive 'p' throughout pleases Paul.
The 'b' of bard bounces brilliantly upon his lips.
Together: baps and Pob cause spittle to fly.
Why oh why cause spittle to fly,
perhaps I'll...

Write.

First person slips in.
Change of narration. Tone. Focus.

Be.
Write again.
Be.

Reading an Audience

'Now I'm not racist but...' is how it begins:

I'm judging what will work

And what will (for my sins)

Not.

Work.

Some of you don't

And some of you do.

Some of you work every hour god sends

And some may have two

Or three or many

Gods

Some none.

When I write, and perform

Words

I tap into relatable identifying thoughts
Ideas of the many, ideas that have been caught
Into media consumed

Media rejected

Media repeated

Hegemonically perfected

Into culture.

Society

Appeal to the masses

Who is Anansi?

Not taught in our classes

We have Christ. We have Arthur
We have Robin Hood
We don't know the Vedas
But perhaps we should?

Writing, and performing

Requires one to understand

Where you stand. Where they stand

Upon whose shoulders, which land

Which myth, which culture to tap into

Appropriately

(Mis-appropriate at your risk)

The youngsters google "what is a floppy disk?"

Save icons for the future and learn from the past;
History repeats but the poet's voice lasts.

P IS FOR POETRY

Alliteration and assonance are for any arrangement

Bards begin to hook an expectation

Create the connotation.
Colours and creatures conspire for symbolic meaning...

Deconstruct these symbols to understand?
Destroy? Desire? Deepen?

Exaggerate and emphasise!

Force a rhyme, half the time, to chime the climate of vogues.

Go.

Hai-ku: measuring / Syll-a-bles for some con-ceit
/ A mess-age con-vey-ed

Implied? Inferred? I think I imply that you infer my eye is first.

"Just a joke though" Context and jest jostling for justice

Knowledge of the silence. The K is key.

Look at line length: Limerick:5 – Long epic-late result.

Metaphors change not the simile. The I in smile is lost
I=am mal=le=a=ble: Magical. M-O-O-N spells 'moon'.

Nearing a conclusion now, notice the nuance. Tone. Change.

Onomatopoeia to alert, to shock, awaken...

Pop!

P is for poetry

Mingling

(For those with worries about being equally nice to others.)

How do you do?
My name is and My job is and My life is
All defined in a few sentences.
We summate and gestate and gesticulate
Our lives
Before moving onto the next.

Into a few lines.

A few lines of text, well-rehearsed, well repeated.
Well-rehearsed
Well repeated:

How do you My name is I am a
Done.
Easy when you know how.
If you're one of them.

A *mingler.*

Mingler: Noun, properly attired –
A breed of person that is not yet fully developed
Evolves into:
into an extrovert
A party animal
or (Heaven forbid)
A *host.*

It starts with the children's party.
(I say the children's party but
it is the adult's party organised for the child by
the parent for the other parents to show how well
they have worked, so hard, at being a parent.
Look at me, I am successful. How do *you* do?)

The child looks around, anxious.
Friends they have invited?
Maybe. If the love is strong.
Entertainment they like?
Hopefully, if the love is aware.
Food and music and colours and invites and streamers and iced rings
and, and...
It's expected, love.

A child has to learn how to mingle, to blend, to be friendly.
Welcome to my home. I like your home.
Do your best, love. I'll just be over here, love.
"Lovely party".

We pass the parcels of expectation from one parent to the other
We freeze with the music choices correctly, while one by one the
chairs are removed.
We expect the children to know the rules because we know the
rules
Don't we, lovely party, how do you do I am a...
Where is the bathroom please?

"You'll always find me in the kitchen at parties."

Mingling is not on the curriculum and there are no rules of
engagement
(Geneva has yet to list the child's party in its treaties)

I'm worried.
I don't want to play with the others
I don't want to play with their toys
They might not like me
They may not want me
How long will it last
Will there be cake
I'm allergic to
I don't want to
Why do I have to
Where is the
Did you bring the

The child, overwhelmed, anxious
Cries the night before.
(It isn't made any easier when their body has grown though)
The mingling has yet to be taught
The rules are still unwritten

You just muddle through, love.
Do your best, love.

How do you do?

"Lovely party".

A Pregnant Pause

The sex, I assume, was good.
Past now though. Agreed upon.
Parent. Parent. Word. Rhythm. Now.
Now I am pregnant.

The idea has gestated. Formed.
Embryonic at first, it was fed, has fed off of me and has now grown inside me…
But I need it out now.

Is it time?

I push. This is not shit. I want this life to grow.
It cannot be forced.
Sometimes, I feel, stroke it, then desire to cut it out.
It is getting bigger, weighing me down. Swelling.
My brow sweats, A false labour.

Contractions. Formalities of informal interactions.
Count the breaths. Push.
The muse paces outside, awaiting the news. Push.

Give me DRUGS! Help me! Get out! Stay. Hold me. I need you here.
(parents and partners and other children are confused in this time of creation) Push.

Midwife metaphor mops my brow. Holds my hand. Removes the pen. Allows me a pause.
Then encourages once again.

Push.

Breathe.

Write.

RED TAPE

"Britannia, that unfortunate female, is always before me, like a trussed fowl: skewered through and through with office-pens, and bound hand and foot with red tape."

David Copperfield, Charles Dickens

N.H.S. Stealing

So

I have an issue with the N.H.S.

Quite a few actually. Six, possibly seven in fact.

I'm ignoring the fact that the nurses, the doctors, the support staff throughout are tired. Worked out. Are amazing.

I'm ignoring the fact that they have to take it, not like that, from every direction with idiots of the public.

And I'm ignoring the fact that their pay does not reflect their hard work.

I'm ignoring the fact that, day after day, they are continually ignored, their voices unheard, their value undervalued, and their support mechanisms depleted.

I'm trying to ignore the fact that they are awesome.

Because I have these issues you see.

I'm upset because they stole the rainbow from us.

The rainbow – we, the gays, took it from the straights and the orthodox religions where it was a sign of universal love to show how love could be universal.

And what have you done with it?

What have you made it into.

Oh.

A sign of universal love.

Where every single person who comes through an emergency door in this country is helped.

Where every single person, regardless of their gender, their body, their love, their blood, is helped.

(and yes, I know some of the staff are still learning, but heck aren't we all? I mean, if I don't know a person's gender, what do I call them now?!)

Where every single person, married person, poly relationship person, asexual person is treated with dignity.

Oh – sounds like I have found a pot of gold.

This universal love thing? Is it always found with a rainbow?

Pink Pounded

Rainbow it

It makes it gay!

We can sell it to them more then!

Those people.

Them

The ones we want the money from.

The ones who have more money

(Well they used to

Times are harder.

Even the gays are feeling the pinch)

Remove the green now, the leaves and recycled imagery.

Time for multicolour.

We'll use the other side of the bunting.

What's next?

Cancer? Charity something?

Oh. That history month.

Let's just repeat what we did last time...

The Second Key Stage

Teacher, Master, Sir
Hierophant, Psychopomp
Holder of secrets
Gatekeeper of knowledge
Assessor, Examiner, Invigilator
Head
Burdened shoulders
Knees
Toe the line.
Get schooled;
Learn words;
Learn patterns.
Learn facts and dates and repeated opinions.
The key is not just to open the door.
But to decide whether or not the door is the right one to go
through;
Or if it should be left.
Check the colour.
The paint, the engravings and markings
The runes and etchings and moonlit messages.
Say friend, speak now of what you want to learn.
Your time for exams is over.
The doors have been opened for you
(So long as you were given a key to begin with)
No key? No worries.
There are many doors to open.
Those who can teach, do.
Those who can't?
Learn.

Anxious Bliss

The trees are not socially distanced.

The river has not been flow-tested.

The birds and butterflies are not masked.

I am still.

The stones are not being counted.

The rate of tree growth is not measured.

The sky is not isolated.

My environment is still.

My mother is still vulnerable,

I am still responsible.

Society is still accountable.

Nature is still.

Will You Belong?

Hi. Can you hear me?

Do you understand me – I'm like you – you're like me yeah?

Yes? Correct? Is that a correct assumption?

We're all the same, all in the middle, desiring Maslow's triangular needs.
Just the exterior is different etc.

Our hair colour. Our eyes.

 And the gender.

Sex.

Skin colour.

Religion.

Viewpoints on political stances.

Sexual orientation and disabilities and nationality and heritage and language and all of the other tick-boxes that separate us.

Divide us.

United we tick, divided we… tick.

"Let's discriminate positively people."
Let's *all* do it – so we *all* belong to the groups organised by the groups who want us to belong to the groups that they want to put us in.

Tick-Boxes.

     Tick-Cages.

          Tick-Camps.

Square boxes made legal and tied up with a nice red tape bow.

Our society is good. We all belong here. All of us who were born here that is.
Not them though. Not those people.

Well unless we asked them, Windrushed them for our pleasure, her majesties pleasure.
Gave them papers then lost them to say thank you.

But not the other ones. They don't belong here. Them. You know, those people.

The people whose food we eat, run the shops we buy our milk and beer in. Kick the balls for our nation. The people taking our jobs, the people who don't belong here anymore.

The ones that don't belong.

You know them, don't you?

The racists.

The sexists and homophobes and bigots.

The hash-tag-haters

They don't belong.

But they do though, don't they?

Because our tolerance of intolerance is complicit. We've ticked it away already.
We've given them our data. We've told them how we different we all are in order to be like the others.

So we can belong with everyone else.

Orange skin on TV directs our attention,
On a love island, In a white house.
Vote for them. Don't. Doesn't matter – they'll have the media eating up their produce.

Want to belong?

Eat.   It.   Up.

Be a good consumer and belong.

Or don't.

Be short.

Be short tempered. Don't be patient. Don't consume their words.

Be short with your time and with your fuse.
Argue.
Make your voice heard.

For while you have a yam in your mouth and your doors aren't knocked on

Speak out.

They will come.

You won't be-long will you?
Because it's not just me waiting...

Distances in Social Media

I'm looking for a green dot.
Can you help me?
There are black dots and spots marking those that
Should not be here
Are not here.
Red crosses on doors
White crosses where red once were.
Red dots of stand by
Red and yellow lights signalling me to stop and stand by
Spelling out warnings in messages by the road

I'm alone.

There are people near me but not close.
Red, white and blue through their veins
But I'm looking
Looking for a green dot
To say it is ok to approach.
They are here too.
They are online.
Looking
Needing
Wanting to stay away from the other dots.
The ones that mean
They are not here.

I am lonely.

I'm looking for a green dot.
Are you here as well?

Pathogen of Least Resistance

Rinse your hands
20 seconds
I'm lazy

Social distance
6 feet, apart
I'm lazy

Reduce contact
Safety first
I'm lazy

Stay inside
Protect yourself
I'm lazy

Mother's day
Easter Sunday
I'm lazy

Government
Voting records
I'm lazy

NHS
Claps and cut backs
I'm lazy

Where's the cops?
Where's the funding?
Are they lazy?

Coughing lots
High temp and fever
Now I'm worried...

Test me now
Not enough Sir
Now I'm unknown

Figures rise
So do worries
Now I'm in bed

Not a sick bed
Tucked in death bed
Rest in peace now.

UNITY

(The state of being united or joined together as a whole or blank)

The dichotomy is not lost on he, the bard-wannabe
The paradoxical "how can one be all" chanting through his head
Dumas' Musketeers echoing barks from 80's children's themes.

One for all and all for ...

One in 10?

The Victorian natured lesbian who is the head of a school
who has her lover as her deputy
who is not known
not 'out'
to her students
Sits as one as part of her team with her students.

Just in case

The sodomite who works with your children
Teaching children the filth that are the lies of their agenda
They are everywhere and will infiltrate
Make people proud to be sinful
Not one but 28
Report them.

Just in case

The greedy bisexual who is almost in tears
Teaching in the mainly Muslim school
(The terrorists and fundamentalists in training – them, you know)
Crying because?
When asked what the issues with same-sex marriage and same sex
adoption were

His students answered with a science question not a social one
or a moral one or an ethical one

They have no issue or concern
Well, just one: *"How do they feed a baby if they're two men?"*

Just, in case

She sits, serving customers in the supermarket
Her larger hands and lower voice identifying her
as one
One who is different, who can be laughed at, pointed at
One who just wanting a job, to transform her life, to earn money, 'to help'

Every. Little. Helps.

Just.

These questions are raised every day in the community
These numbers of Kinsey's devising, of modern surveys
He sits wanting her pronouns to be recognised while she is a man
She sits wanting her pronouns to be recognised as a
He/She sits while
Heshe sits
They sits
They sit

One does not simply walk into pronouns

Just In Case.

A poet stands at a microphone
An audience listen to his one voice
They are part of a whole while he
He, They

Sit…

Stand as one.

Just. In. Case.

RED ON YOU

"You've got red on you"

Shaun of The Dead, Edgar Wright, Simon Pegg and Nick Frost

Scales – Skin and Sound

There is a snake of darkness above my head

On my scalp to be exact in my scalp?

I propose that this supposition of the preposition creates an opposition or juxtaposition that exposes the repose of a creature not as feature but as leech-er. Nietzsche. Skaoi. Vanessa

Names are important.

(Though I am sure it is a sister of the serpent that sits in my cerebellum – It is not the Skaldic _word_ serpent but certainly seems a huge monster indeed)

Names are important.

To define is to delineate and to describe and to descale this situation. To seize control and I so need control of her.

Her serpent's name is Psoriasis, and she slithers around giving me presents. Small scabs and scales of darkness that gestate into smaller snakes that bite their own tales.

Psoriasis: I name thee.

Growing extra skin

Skin for me to pick at, to scratch at, to slew.

Each time I remove a piece of my scalp, scratching another line in the sand, another notch on the noggin, the smile that she shares with me fuels her tenacity and she supplants another piece onto my scalp, another idea to be picked at.

Psoriasis: I conjure thee.

I'm looking through Wikipedia articles looking for 's' words to encourage this sibilance of sorcery. Scouring and seeking and searching through serpentine imagery and Skaldic stories and tales of tails that slither on scalps.

Psoriasis: I bind thee.

The information that is certified is now denied to enter my head. The scales on my scalp and her skin merge causing a shield that centres around my uncertainty yet my certainty that this information causes her sorrow sears her ideas into my head further. But the seers amongst my peers have been here before and been with her before and have named her before and limited her before as before me there were others.

On the shoulders of psoriasis sufferers I stand.

The serpent is inside this enclosure of sounds and of seemings. She is now encircled, enslaved; defining her power now limits her, she glowers and cowers and lowers her guard thus limiting her.

Limiting her sorcery is this poem's aim.

This spoken word's aim.

For there is no structure to this seeming semblance of sounds

Just arrogance and sibilance and sarcasm.

Sibilance from 'sibilare' to hiss that I had missed this last century that this piss taking of my own serpent scalp, the snakes that Medusa had are not similes but metaphors and are now becoming ...

Real.

Do I mean that her petrification of this realisation and personification of this alliteration is suddenly sensible?
Does. It. Make. Sense?

Am I just showing off the fact I have studied and remedied and found a dictionary of rhyming for this timing of the piebald fact I am miming and pacing my way through this spoken piece.

Psoriasis: I name thee.
Psoriasis: I conjure thee.
Psoriasis: I bind thee.

Not with the entrails of my daughter that I have slaughtered but with the ties of the lies that I realise I lie with daily. Nightly. Hourly. Mi – newt-ly.

No longer will her serpent's poison drip into my mind's eye but the bowl held by my spouse (my masculinised Sigyn) as they collect.
As they pour, pause with paws held out, eager to help but unable to save me from the scale of this serpent.

It is named.
It is conjured.
It is bound.

To dismiss then this hiss then. To kiss away then this pain that she causes while pauses occur with a bowl over my head. She is dead to me. My scalp is no longer her nest for her rest, the rest of her fellow thought vipers. It is now a place for her decrease, to desist, to decease. I resist her insistence. I end her.Psoriasis. You are dismissed. My will is stronger than yours.

You. Have. No. Power. Over. Me.

BROTHERS

There is always an older one
Which in turn defines a younger one.
Age is irrelevant until experience rears its head
Challenges the other.

Blood from a parent, maybe two
Flows through both.

Genetic links that intertwine
Like fingers at a funeral
Like arms and looks between older men
Like memories that are formed by parents
and missing people
and death.

We are all brothers, us men, when we lose a female relative.
The women know how to weep, to talk, to express.
The men become united in grief in their silence.
We are brothers of the quiet respect until one chooses to show
To offer brotherly advice
To cry.

Brotherly love shown not just with blood bonds
But salt-tear bonds.
Harder to form, harder to break.
Blood and still waters run deep but tears
Tears flow along Rome's roads, Eden's highways and along
Asgardian myths.
Brothers are always different but we all wipe our tears away as one.

Parasites

It starts with an itch.

Something that cannot be scratched, reached, realisation that
that
that there is something that cannot be reached. Achieved.

Siphonaptera

The cat scratches itself whilst the little blood sucking flea jumps
ever higher
on its back, onto the table, onto my arm, onto the sofa
and back again.

Once seen, you know it's there.
You look for it, to desire its death, its eradication from your world.

To crush between fingernail and thumbnail.

You itch.

Pediculus humanus capitis

The headlice that crawls on the child's head
your head
the regretted day of supply teaching, of picking up the friend's child,
of babysitting, of the seat on the bus next to scratchy family
the sharing is caring
but not with public enemy parasite number 1
Tea tree oil will not stop the itching
the thinking
the thinking of itching
the thinking of thinking of itching of whether you are thinking to itch
because you are thinking of itching or whether you have lice and if
you do then do you itch or does that...

You itch.
You itch until you get the itch.
Focus on something else.
You itch a little less, knowing that you… No.
Don't think about it again.
(Itching yet?)

You look at your fingers.
An idea is a parasite. It feeds off you. The itch doesn't go away.
We must remove parasites unless they serve a purpose.
They come into our space, feeding, taking from us, demanding our
focus. How dare they, the…

Homo Sapiens

Parasites.

The expectant mother looks at her swelling belly,
Swelling with pride, with blood, with feeding child, with the new
member to their family with eighteen years, with change with new
change, with old life being lost with

with

Itch

Children running around in the park, smiling, happy, cheerful,
dancing, renewed energy, ever regenerating.
But where do they get their energy from?

Look at the drained carer, the fatigued teacher, the patient bus
driver, the tired parent.
They smile too, but it is a tired smile.
A smile that hides the itching.

SAMARITANS

(Not just for the suicidal)

No. They're not – they help and prefer to help people *before* they get to that state. Growing up a depressive in a small, isolated town wasn't easy. There was Childline for the under 18s – but what then? – I felt too bad to take up their time so who to turn to. No one for a while. Then, then I needed someone to listen. To listen to my issues.

The Samaritans listened.

When my life started falling apart at university, I needed someone to listen. It was 3 in the morning. I was at the door of change: my life could have gone in many ways, many of them being negative.

Someone needed to be there – it was 3 in the morning though. Who to call? Who to listen?

The Samaritans listened.

When a relationship failed, but everyone knew both of us – when I was in a small community, when I couldn't talk about it to my best friend because they knew the other half, wouldn't have been impartial, wouldn't have cared, would possibly have blamed, judged... I needed impartiality.

The Samaritans listened.

I have been at the edge of despair. I was held back, not by hands but by an ear. A shoulder to lean on.

Someone cared.

Someone volunteered, gave up their time, for whatever reason and listened, through sensitive training, through careful managed listening techniques but ultimately through empathy, sensitivity and love for another human on this spinning rock through space

They listened.

The Samaritans listened.

Thank you, volunteer, for listening to someone.

It might not seem much at the time, but I know, I KNOW that I wouldn't be here today writing this, having helped other people, helped tutor others, teach others and train others in knowledge and basic skills were it not for the fact that, at 3am, at a dark point in my life – on a rainy day when all light was not visible...

The Samaritans listened.

Thank you for listening.

Stickers

I

It started with a kiss.

Possibly. But I don't remember.
I DO remember a sticker though.
An adhesive acknowledgement
A decal demonstration of dental hygiene.
"I brushed my teeth!" Smiley toothbrush face.
I was five.
I proudly placed it on the bathroom mirror.
By my toothbrush.
And my teeth.

Slowly.

Rotted.

Because I had done it. I didn't need to do it again. Or again.
Once the certificate, the star, the sensation of success had been solidified...
I moved on.
Why achieve the same thing again? And again?
This continued.
To others I became lazy in tasks
Asking for proof was not needed.
School was not concerned. They had their proof.
The pudding of Paul was all purposed. Proven.
The academic spoon had stirred. My mixtures? Marvellous.
But Christmas comes but once a year – my yearning for yule-time pudding
Was daily.

Showing off. Attention seeking. Not now. Too talky. Too chatty.

*"I live for the **applause, applause, applause**…"*

Drama and wordplay danced deliriously close to hedonistic dangers
(Another story. Another time.
But even at twelve, I understood how adults groom their prey)
We are all prey. We seek our stickers, our acknowledgements.
Pray for someone above us to notice. To award us.
*"I live for the **applause, applause, applause**…"*

II

It started with a kiss.
Teenagerhood became a place of torment.
Who to kiss? When to kiss? HOW to kiss?
There aren't lessons given. Teachers cannot help.
So how do I get my sticker?
What is the mark scheme, the grade criteria?
Who is a good kisser? How do I learn?
Rachel.
New Year's Eve
I was seventeen.
Alcohol.
I did not get a sticker…

III

It started with a miss - ed grade
College and University had new levels.
This I can relate to. New schema. New boundaries.
Stickers are grades and labels of identity.
I wear my identity. Others wear theirs.
My teeth still rot.
I learn new things but...
I. Do. Not. Learn. From. My. Mistakes.
You can get more stickers – if you continue your progress.

Oh.

My teeth stop rotting.
My soul is now certified.

IV

It started with a kiss.
My sticker is one of two.
They are silver. Round.
Finger placed.
Look
I have achieved.
I am proud.
My remaining teeth shine.

V

It starts with a sticker.
We, bards, writers, storytellers, achieve kisses of acknowledgement.
But we cannot live on money alone.
We need **applause. Applause. Applause.**
The irony.
Rainbows faded, nurses tired.
They walk to work on worn out soles.
Our bardic boots still gleam, unused, polished, waiting.
We are zooming about in our slippers, at home.

Alone.

Indoors. Indoors. Indoors.

Muted mics mean our minds become muted.
Our words might get heard;
But we are immune.

We go hungry.
We live for the **applause, applause... applause.**

Seeing Red

"Happily, violence is short lived, only for a very little while do even the gentlest persons 'see red'."

The History of Sir Richard Calmady, Mary St. Leger Harrison (under the pseudonym 'Lucas Malet')

"Would a player mind if he found out a team-mate was gay? Probably. Players wouldn't want to be left alone with him, they wouldn't want to shower with him. Before you rush to criticise, would you find it acceptable for a man to walk around a women's dressing-room? More importantly, team-mates would be self-conscious around the player... Dressing-rooms are like perverted nudist camps. Immature, wild places, little self-contained states where the normal rules of common decency and acceptable behaviour do not apply. "

The Times: "Boys being boys in the dressing-room helps to keep homosexuality in football's closet". (13 Feb 2006), Tony Cascarino, Former Republic of Ireland international.

THERE'S A CRACK IN MY CARAFE
(To the tune of 'There's a hole in my bucket')

My carafe has a crack in
Dear PM, dear PM
My carafe has a crack in
Dear PM, a crack.

    Then fix it, dear voter, dear voter, dear voter,
    Then fix it, dear voter, dear voter, fix it.

With what money should I do it,
Dear PM, dear PM?
With what money should I do it,
Dear PM, what cash?

    With the money left from councils, from funding, dear voter
    The money tree is growing, let's clap and be done.

Can you fix it please PM
Dear PM, dear father?
You lover and dear hero
Who'll never desert...

    Cough cough busy right now friend, dear voter, shaking hands
    cough cough busy right now friend, dear voter, stay close.

Two metres or more now, great leader, great wise man
Experts are telling and saying: What shall we do now?

    Cough cough busy right now friend, cough cough, shaking
    cough cough cough cough busy cough cough cough cough
    cough busy cough.

Who shall stand up now and clap?
Dear PM, Dear PM
Who do we clap for now PM
The keyworkers or you?

Dear PM is busy dear voter, dear voter
Please bear with us voter, things will be ok.

Do we work now or stay in,
dear erm, who should we sing to?
Where do we get our wages now, our bills, rents, mortgage?
The banks will be bailed out, dear voter, don't worry
The airlines and MPs will get money soon.
But the homeless and the starving, is anyone listening
the keyworkers still using food banks it's true.

We'll have more and more money, dear voter, don't worry
Lets not talk politics 10 thousand times no.

There's a hole in my thinking, dear listener, dear voter
Community works only when it is whole.

We've closed down the libraries, the halls and support teams
We've cut back the NHS so much it hurts
We've not listened, invested, protected or sorted
Just reacted and pointed and laughed at the facts
There's a hole in the future dear voter, dear thinker
There's a gap to be filled in let's not overreact
We've excused ourselves plenty dear voter, dear voter
but no one is listening, just dying alone.

COMPETITION

The man sits in the smoke-filled *Earl of Halsbury*

The Sun in one hand
Pint of something dark in the other
Having looked enough at the pictures of page 3, he moves to the
back pages
Always the front, then the back.
That's how you do it.
Flick through.

The competition.

One in ten chance to win.

Mark which player has possession.
Study the picture.
This one taken from the archives.
A well-known match.
First Premier league mixed teams.
Look at them.

Well half of them, if you get my meaning.
Wink, wink, nudge, nudge. Say. No. More.

Liam passes to Lily.
Hope to Aslie.
Casey to Lianne.
Robbie takes it. Retires.
Thomas comes out now, retreating openly.
Megan moves in, drives it forward.
Graeme, misses, distracted by the crowd.
The man picks up his pen.
Marks with a cross.
Justin.

THERE IS NO I IN TEAM

There is no I in team
Or L or G or B
There is a T, so long as you can pass; they don't care how you handle
the balls.
But you're not allowed to go forward,
To progress,
Not while holding it.
You have to aim for the opposite side, the other team.
No aiming for your own, no advantage to be had.
My ankles get tapped, I drop, I run.

Others? They try, of course, they seek conversion.
They crash on, but it's a dummy pass.
The other team, 'them', they know this foul play;
Their heads are on tight, not loose, they understand.

Tonight, the touch is just for the judge.
This set piece... it resets.
We bind and push together.
Can we all move forward?

The whistle blows.
We start the game.

THIMBLERIG [1]

(In the style of T.S.Eliot)

Prologue

Step right up. Where is the card, the lady, the P [2]?

    The bloke [3] smiles at the marks. They watch. They listen.

Is it under the prince's mattress, stopping him sleep?

Keeping him awake at night – where is it, who's taken it?

Appease [4] the linguist, return the missing letter,

Here are three shells – just three of them – mark them.

Watch them.

Place your bets.

Find what you're looking for.

    Hands move. Hands clean. Hands gesture.

    The audience watch.

    One hand reaches forward.

    Another...[5]

C Shell 1 [6]

Carapace of an animal, the protection of an egg

Tread lightly on my thoughts but ravage my flesh?

Eat of this, Our body, your body, my body, *their* body

The Ka [7] is the passenger?

Pleasures of the flesh. Enjoy at your peril.

Shield yourself to the outside world.

The slings and arrows of our enraged fortunes [8] bounce

As we look, we search

Lifting up clothing of stacked upon shells

Trying to open others, clamming up ourselves.

Bodies in the night, slugs making trails.

Remove the shell and we are left with…

Nothing?

see Shell 2

Meryl Streep puts a wig on and another [9]

Hides her money and her skills,

Looks at companies putting boxes in boxes;

Money is moved and hidden and gone.

Panama's papers scatter while leaks are sought quickly.

This ship will not sink but just be jumped over.

Quickly the brown fox ignores the paid off sleeping policemen.

Remove the shell and we are left with...

Another shell?

Subsidiary Shell 3 (see shell 2)

Meryl Streep removes a wig and another,

Reveals her money and her skills.

We look at companies putting money in boxes.

Our money is moved and taken and spent.

Panama's papers are scattered, absorbent.

Soaked up the leaks, they are now tossed in an ocean.

The brown fox has jumped, police numbers cut.

Remove the shell and

...we are left with...

Sorry?

C4 Shell or C Shell 4 or For she sells? [10]

Payloads of explosive packed in tightly,

Pushed in, prodded in, placed in

Payloads

Academics with short fuses and mortar boards

Watch as humanity creates weapons of mass distraction.

Black powder, white powder, flash paper [11], no paper

All distract then detonate then destroy.

Shelled.

Bombed.

Killed.

We hide words and death in terms of maneuverer.

The slings and arrows no match for a gun.

No shield now

Just an empty shell

Remove the shell and we are left.

Sea Shells

Just shells

She has sold them to us. We see on the shore the shells she has sold.

Planispiral Nautilus [12], repeating but ever-expanding.

The universe smiles.

Electrons spinning, dancing,

H and K, letters on a table [13]

Becoming

Just one.

Unity?

A poet sits at home

His quill now a collection of plastic keys
arranged with springs upon electrode inputs
the ink shown by a flashing cursor
awaiting input.

NOTES ON 'THIMBLERIG'

[1] - Thimblerig: The shell 'game' or swindle, where three containers (in the 1790s the containers were thimbles) are mixed around, one hiding a pea or other small item and audience members (usually incorrectly) guess where the pea is.

[2] - P=Phosphorus, (from 'light bearer' aka Lucifer) is essential for life. Life started in many ways in many myths and is searched for continually, many thinking that mythology explains the Big Bang in some manner.

[3] - Bloke is a word meaning man that comes from *Shelta*, a hidden language used by Irish Travellers, possibly derived from loke, Hindi for man which made me think of Loki and gloak, or a variation of gloak from buzzgloak, a pickpocket – all summed up nicely the ideas of the Trickster playing the shell game, wisdom to be found within a game and trick not derivative or against the ideas that they represent.

[4] - The word pea comes from 'pease', with the plural 'peasen' – not pea and pea + s.

[5] - I love the idea of the multiple meanings of the Sistine Chapel's hands of Adam and God reaching for one another can connote.

[6] - C=Carbon, able to form polymers at our planet's temperatures, is the basis for all life. On Earth at least.

[7] - Ka is the Egyptian word for soul but used here to play on the fact that most soul metaphors talk of the body being a shell, a vehicle for the soul and not important in itself.

[8] - Cf. Hamlet Act 3 Sc 1.

[9] - Most of this is referencing the 2019 film *The Laundromat* and its examination of the banking systems of shell companies, insurance fraud and the way that the Panama papers achieved a lot yet did not.

[10] - C4 – a plastic explosive that is mouldable like clay.

[11] - A distraction used by magicians and tricksters – it is made from nitrocellulose and burns quickly and completely with a bright orange flame leaving no ash.

[12] - Planispiral: 'the diameter increases away from the axis of coiling', a great word and one that worked better than 'Fibonacci sequence-esque' or golden ratio etc.; Nautilus is a mollusc that has a shell in a similar pattern, but the image often referred to by mathematicians to explain the Fibonacci sequence/golden ratio. It is also a reference to Jules Verne's ships.

[13] H=Hydrogen, the lightest element and one that makes up ¾ of the universe. It is represented by the atomic number '1', and its graphical symbol is used in many media, notably by Alan Moore in *Watchmen* as the character Dr Manhattan uses it as a 'symbol' cf. Watchmen, Ch.4; K is used here both for Potassium, the element that has one electron in its outer shell and the fact that the letter 'k' is used to denote the shells of electrons themselves. The table is reference to the shell game once again and the overly used periodic table in this poem.

WITH SPECIAL THANKS TO...

-Cover art and internal
illustrations-
Eddie S Ruffles at
Heortlufu Symbolism
heortlufusymbolism@gmail.com

- Photography –
Jack Savage at
The Influx Gallery
www.jacksavage.co.uk

- Editing –
Donna Scott
www.donna-scott.co.uk

... and a big **thank you** for purchasing this book as well.

If you would prefer to consume this book in a different format, please go to: www.paulgiffney.uk/poetry or scan the QR code above.

On the author's website there is an option for you to **listen** to all of the poems from this collection♥, to watch some performed video content and to keep up to date with performances of these, and other, poems.

Please let the author know what you think of it – all criticism is welcome and will help make the next book[s] even better. Email your thoughts to: poetry@paulgiffney.uk .
Paul is available for live performances, writing workshops, and commissioned work as well. Go to the website for more information.

_____

♥ *This audio content will only be available to those who have purchased this book and is a special bonus thank you for everyone supporting Paul.*

BVRSH - #0003 - 160323 - C2 - 210/148/4 - PB - 9781804672648 - Gloss Lamination